Beautiful Designs & Detailed Floral Patterns Adult Coloring Book

By Peaceful Mind Adult Coloring Books

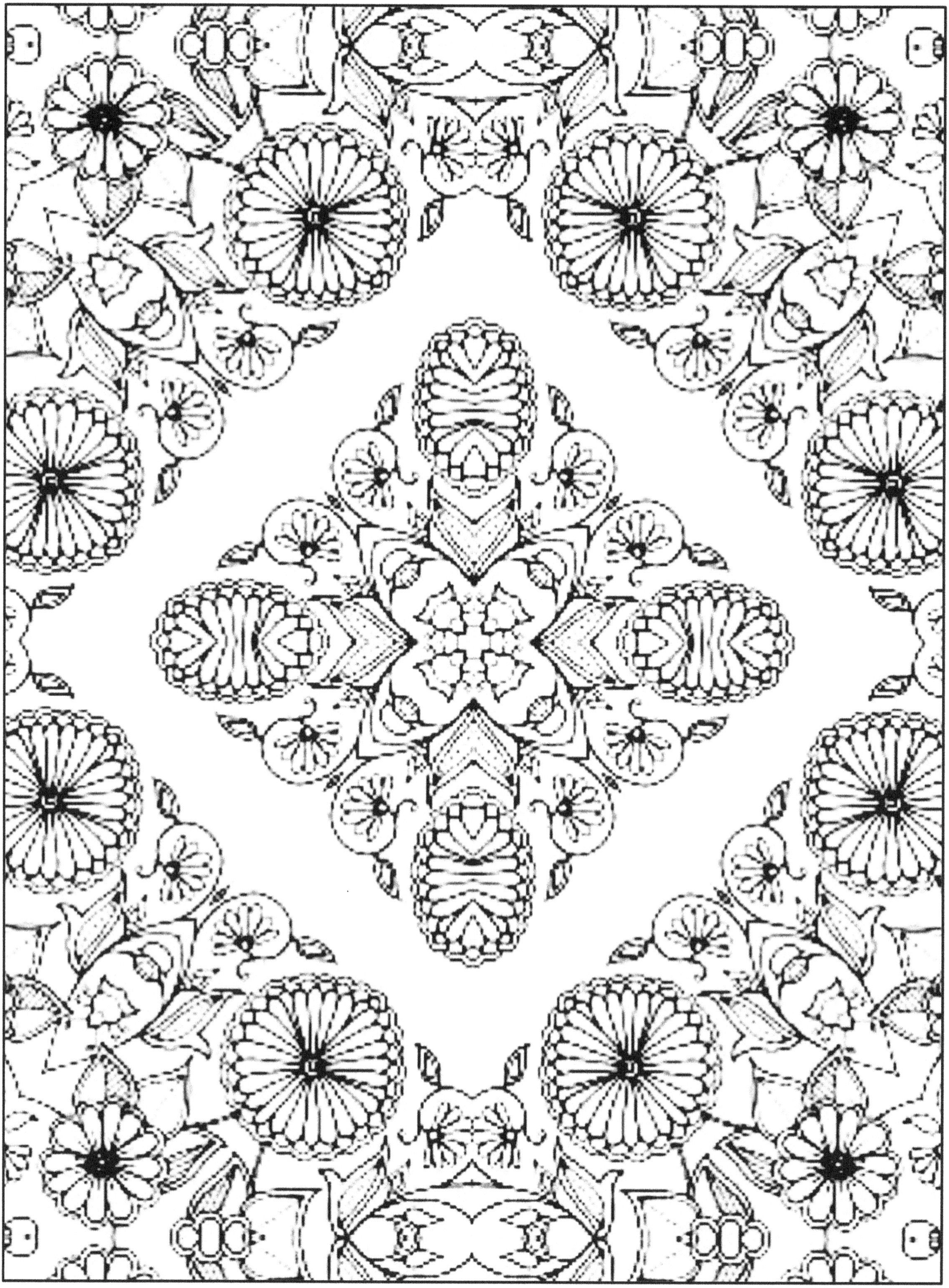

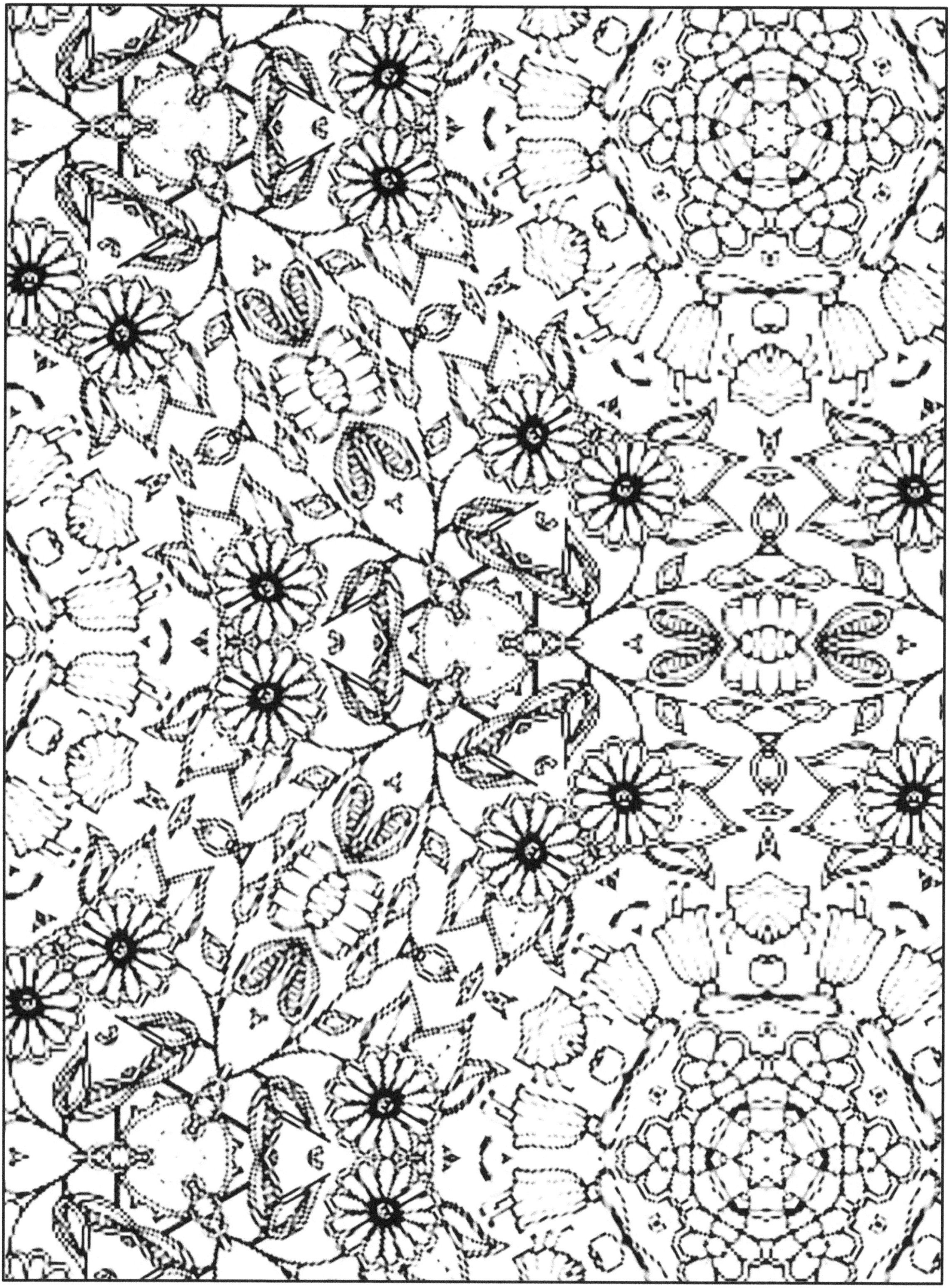

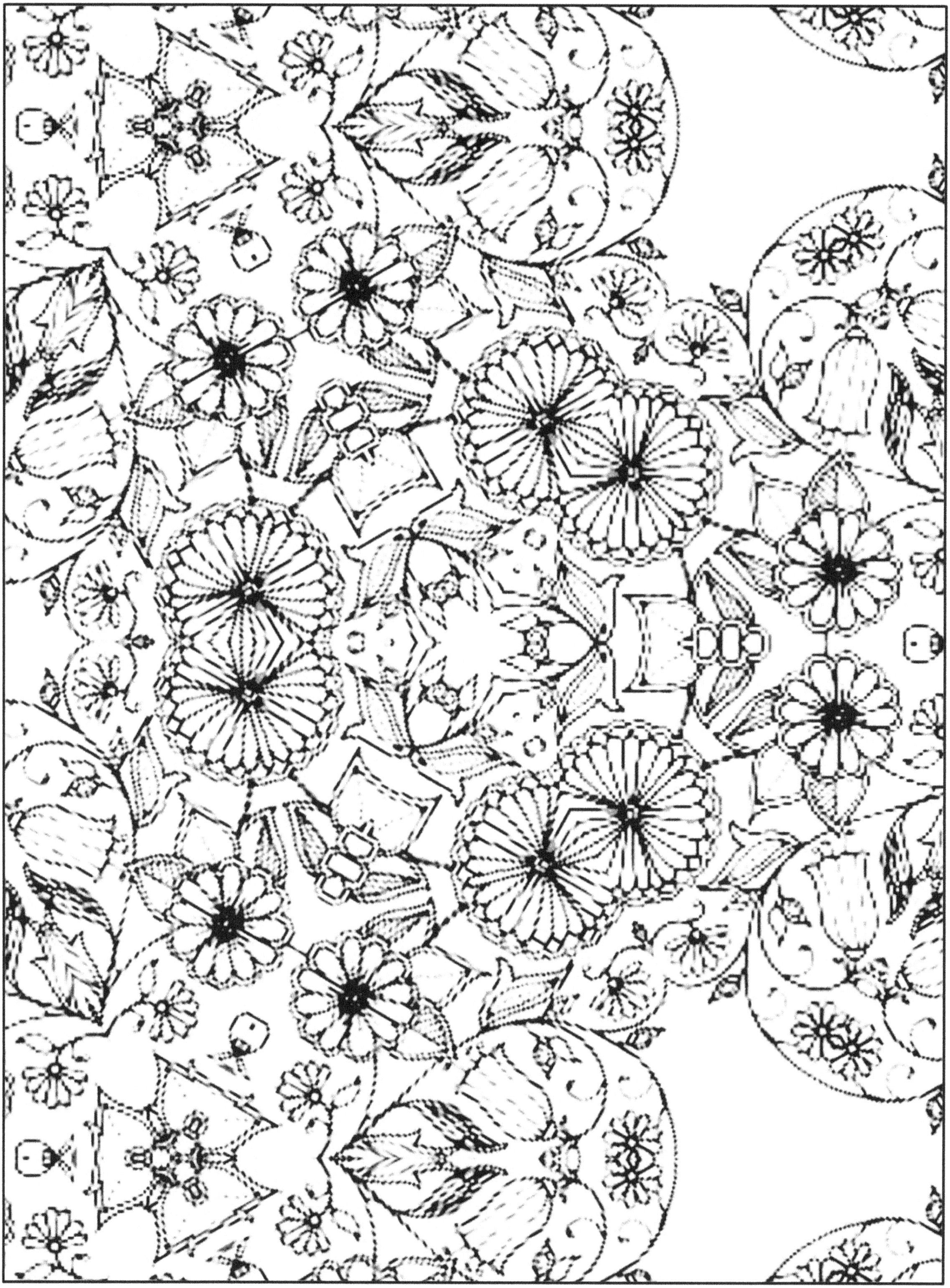

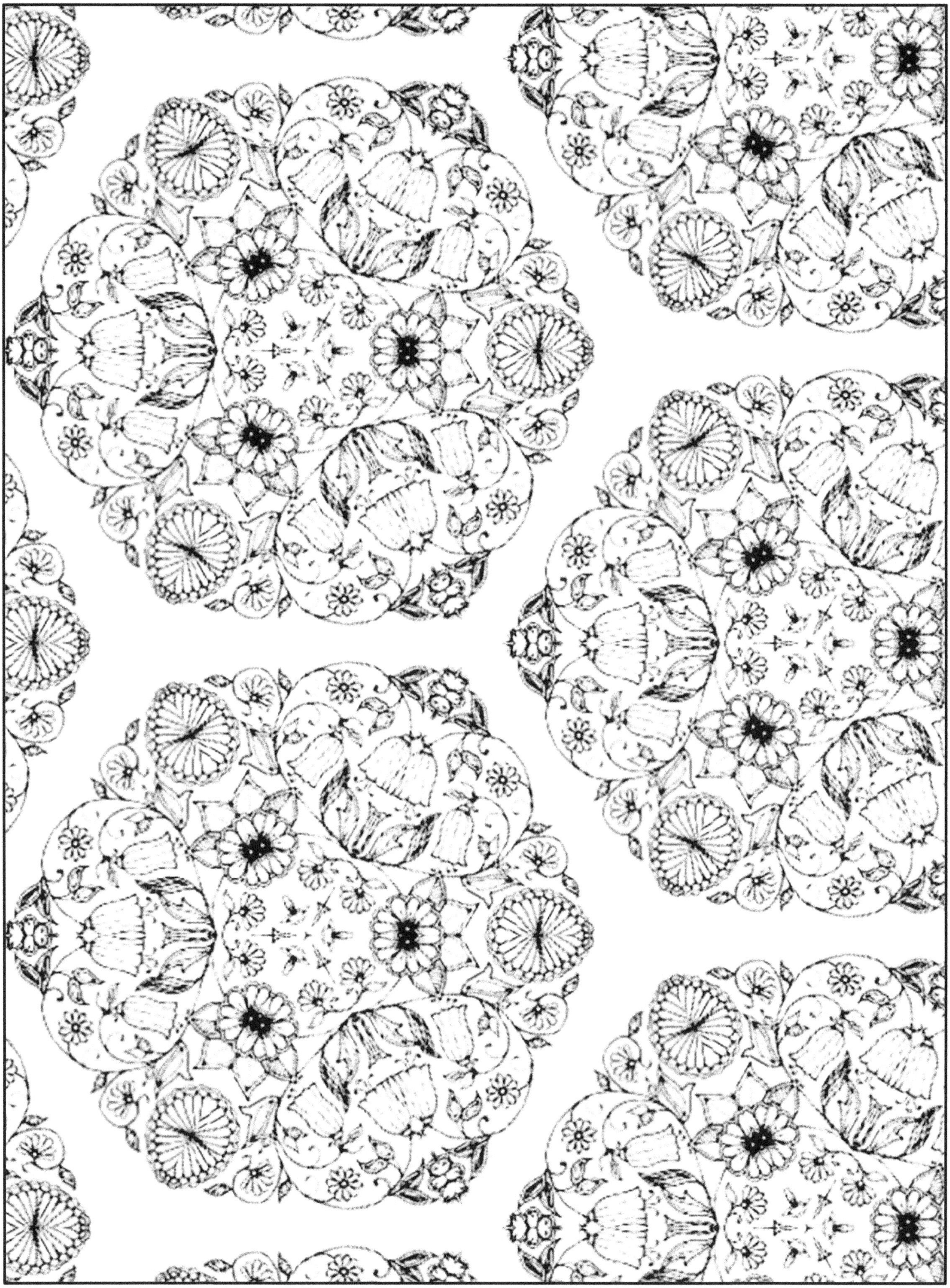

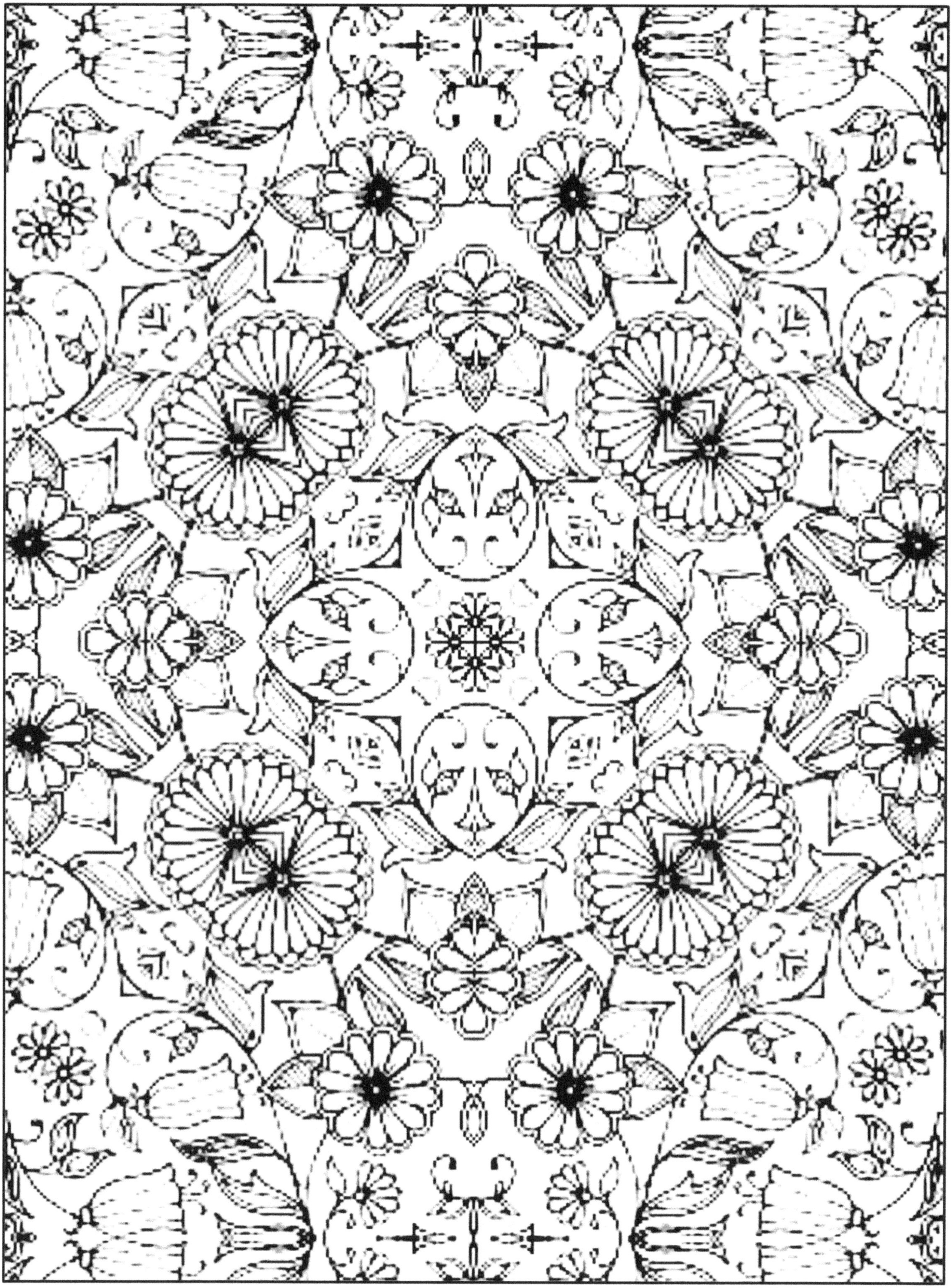

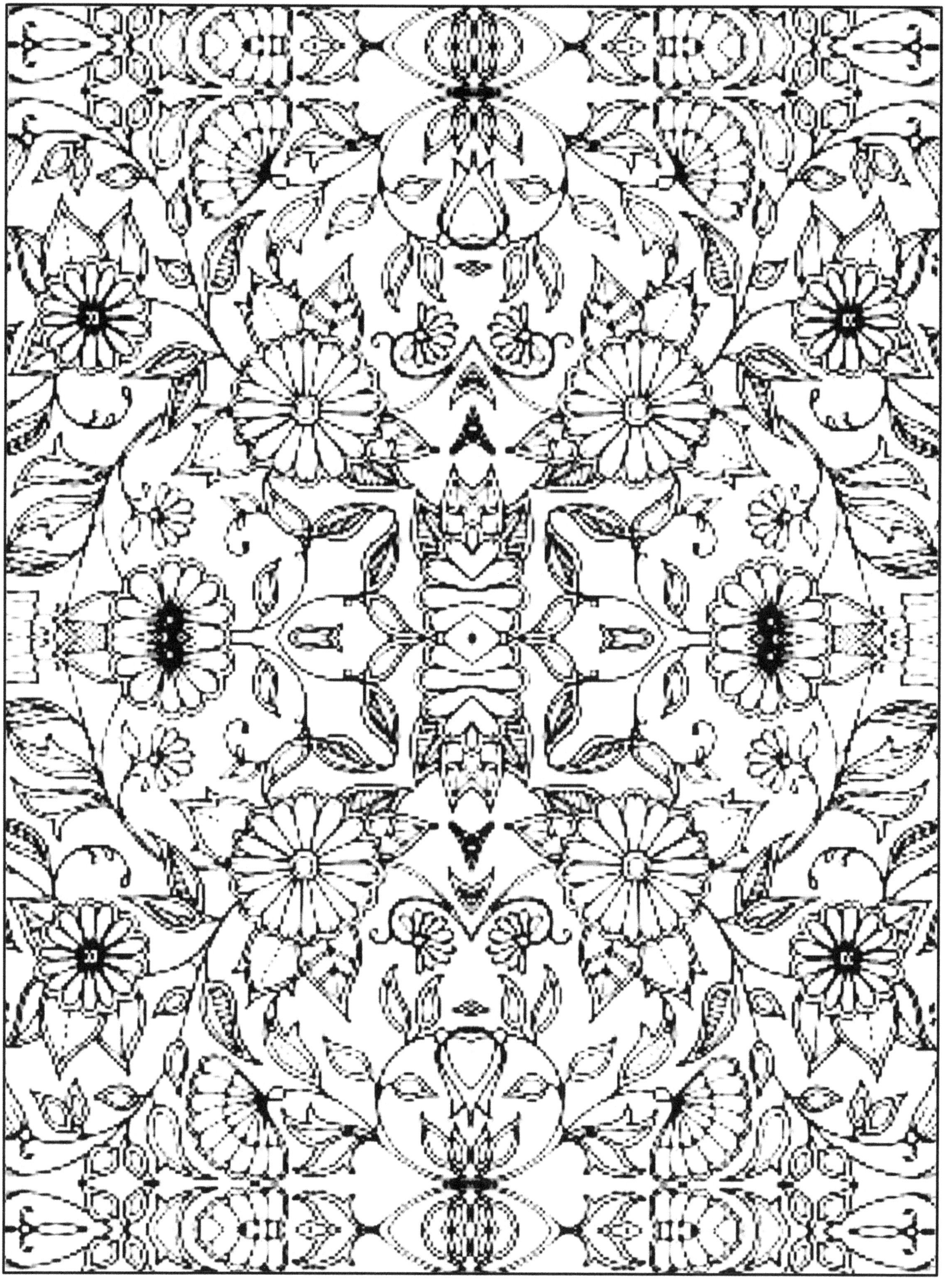

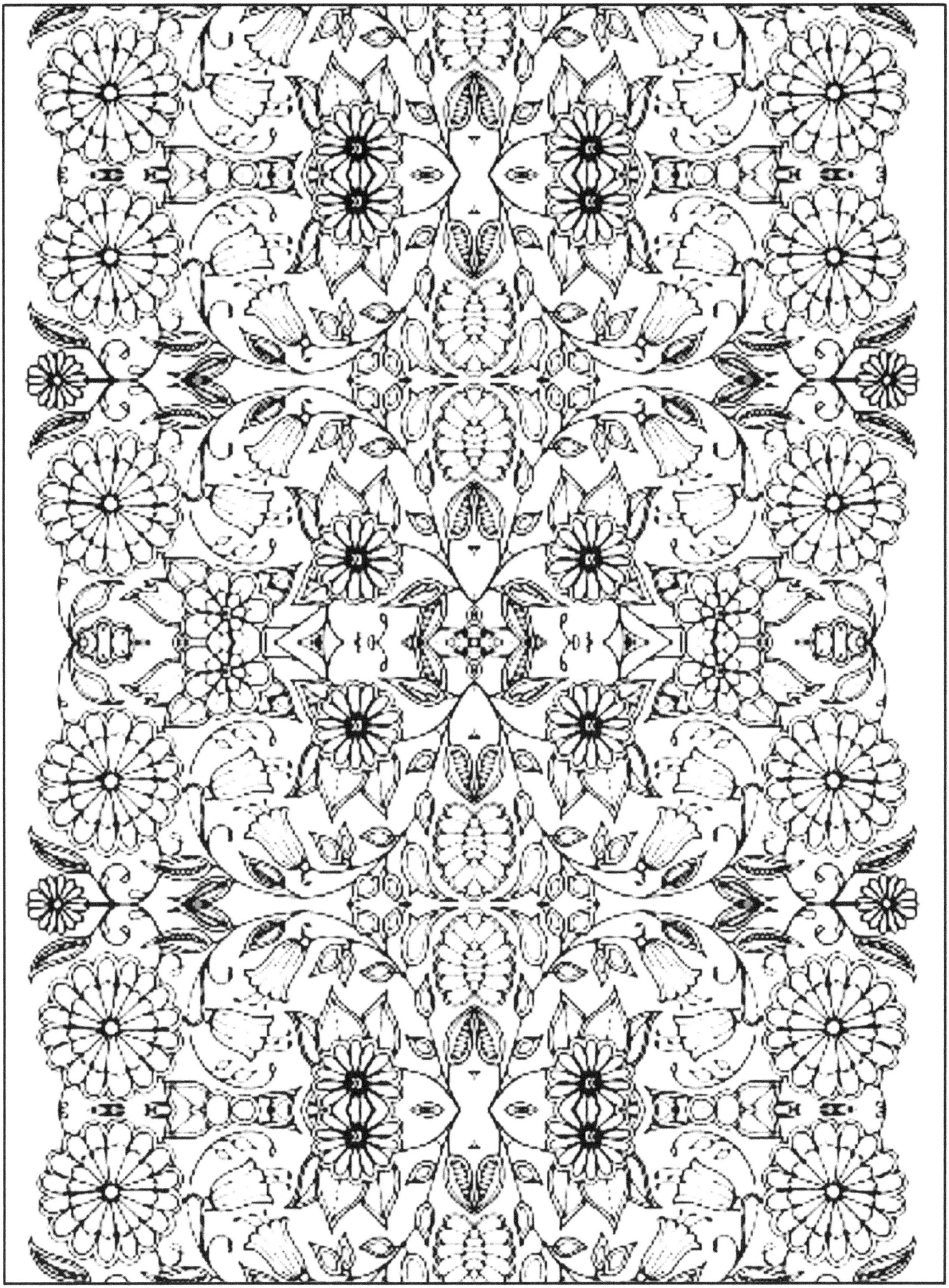

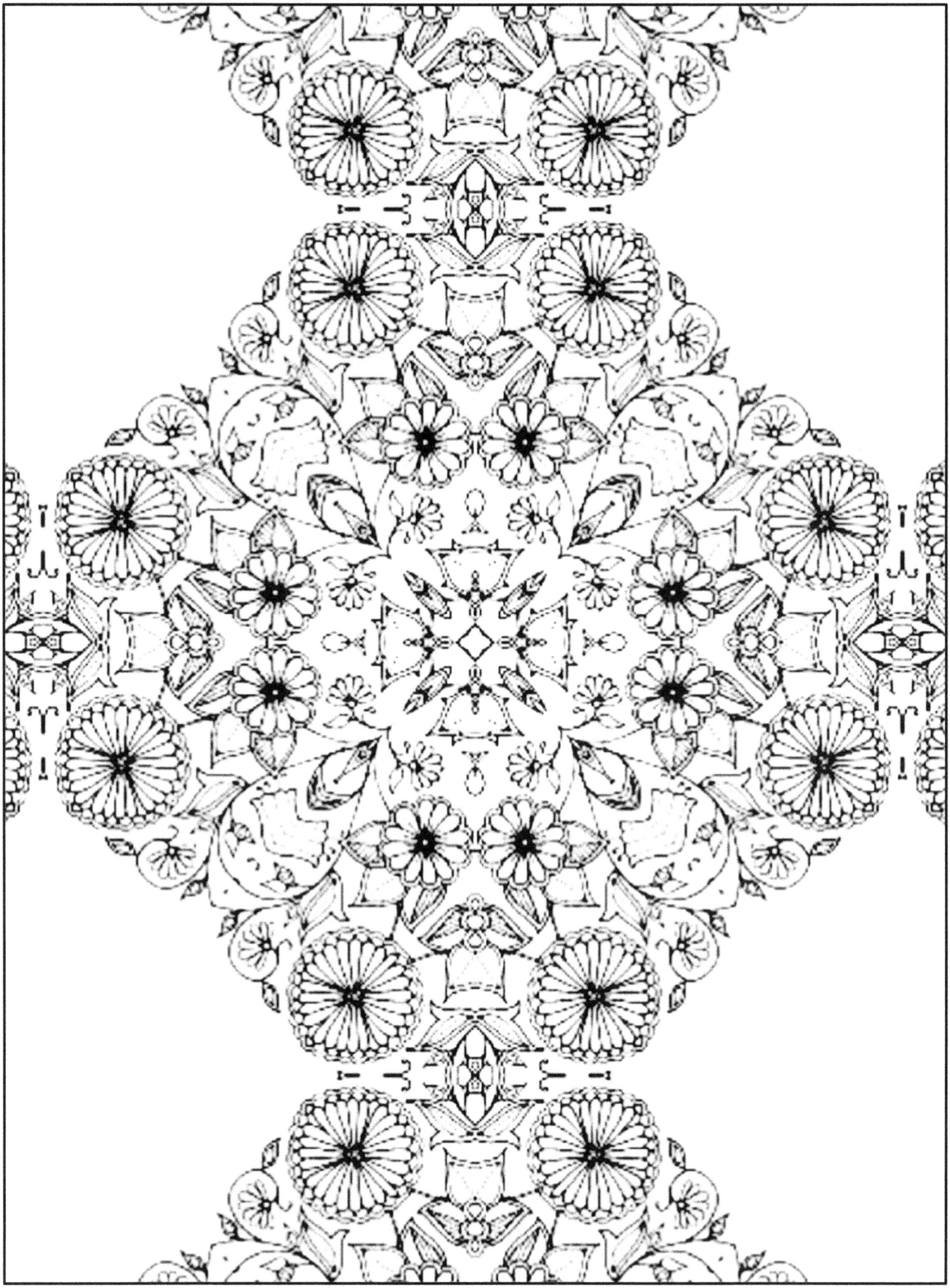

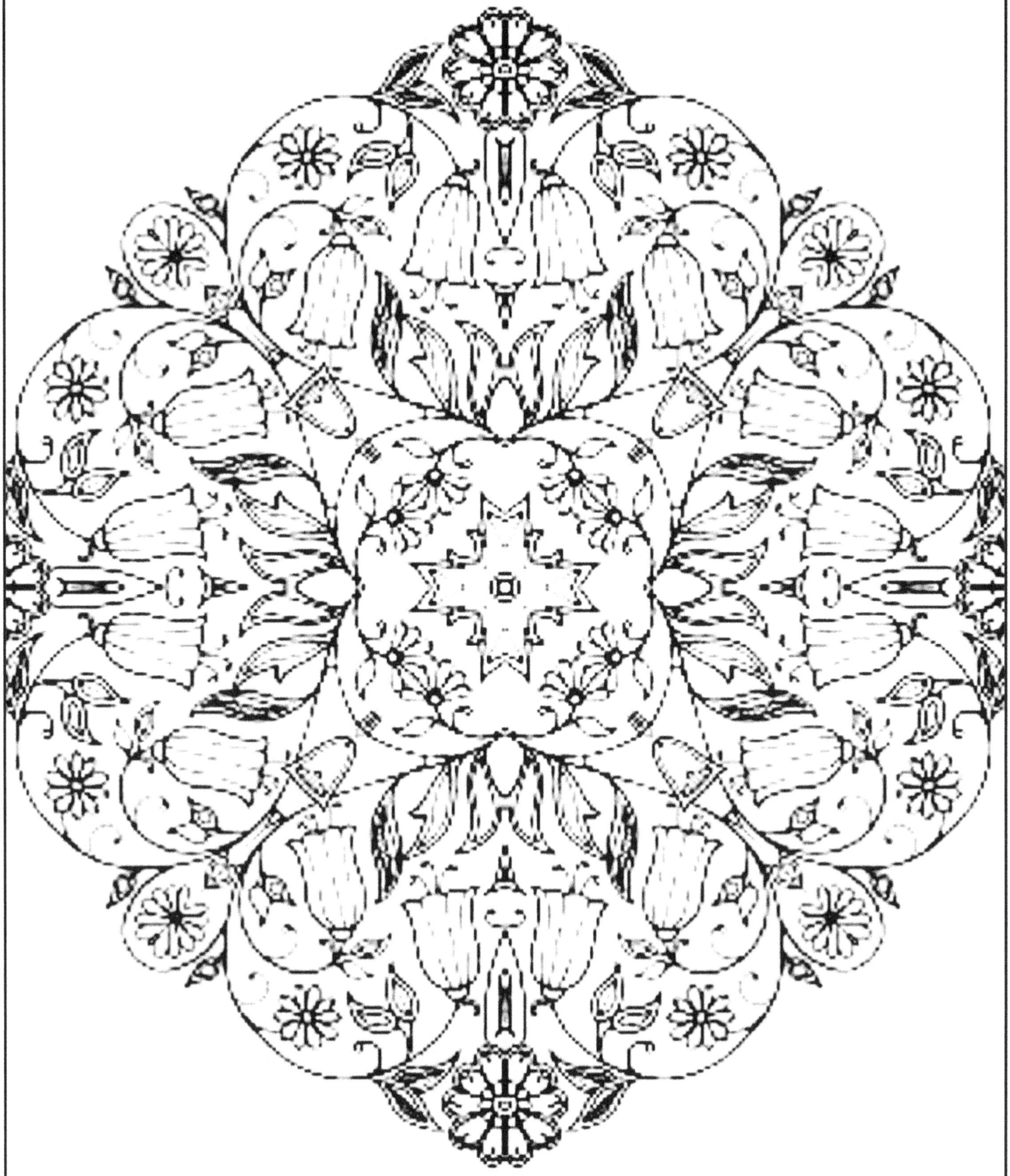

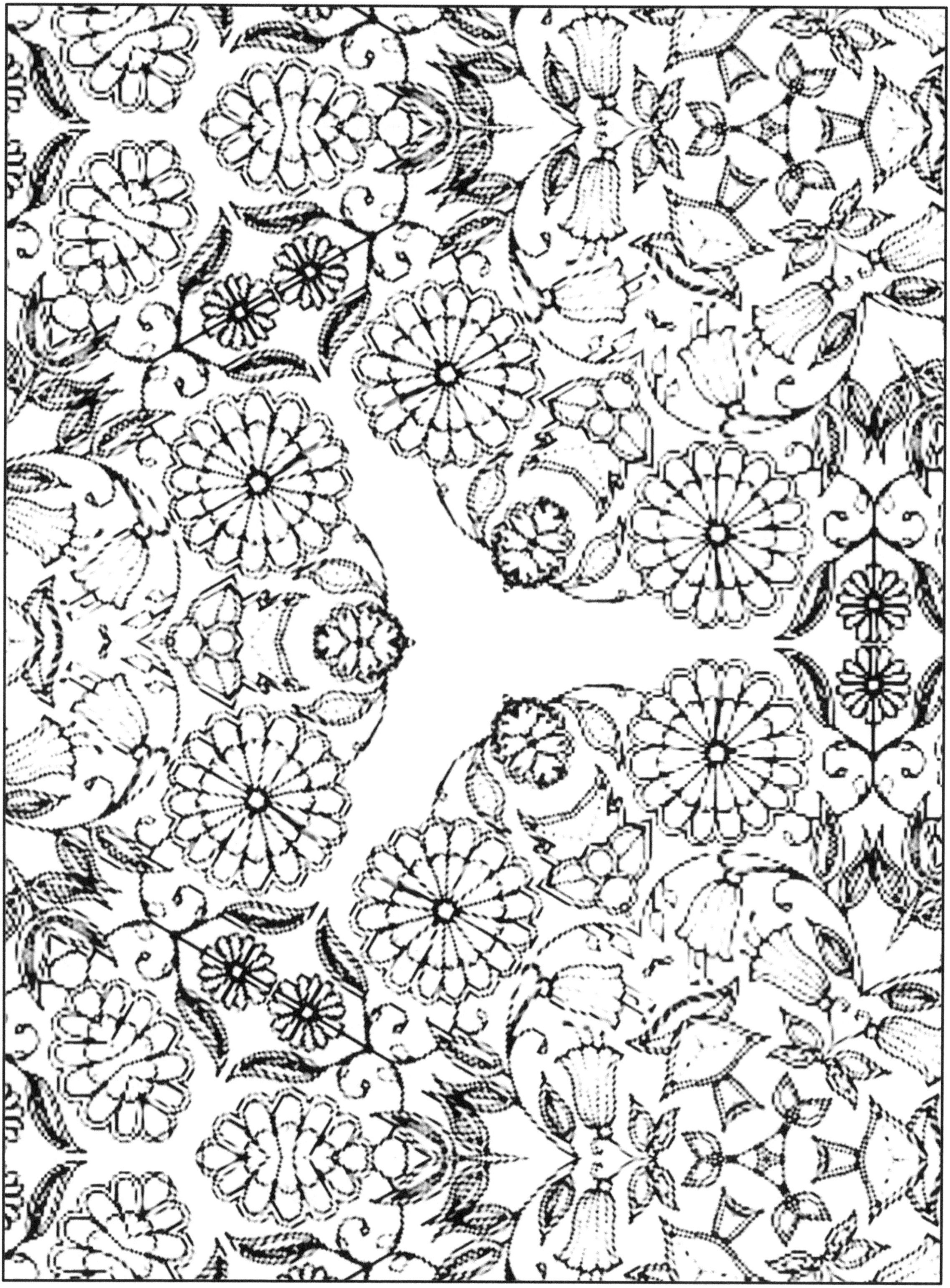

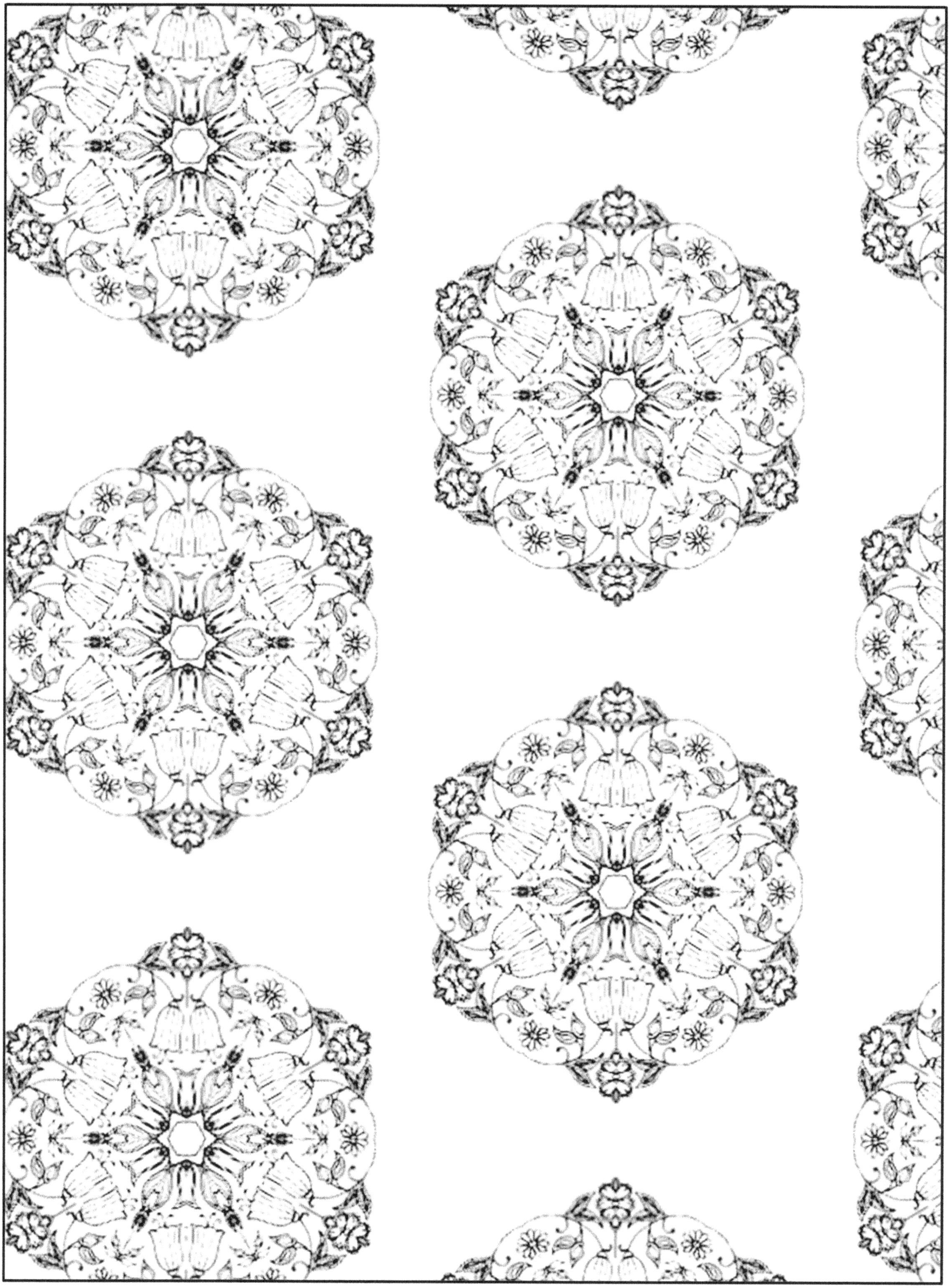

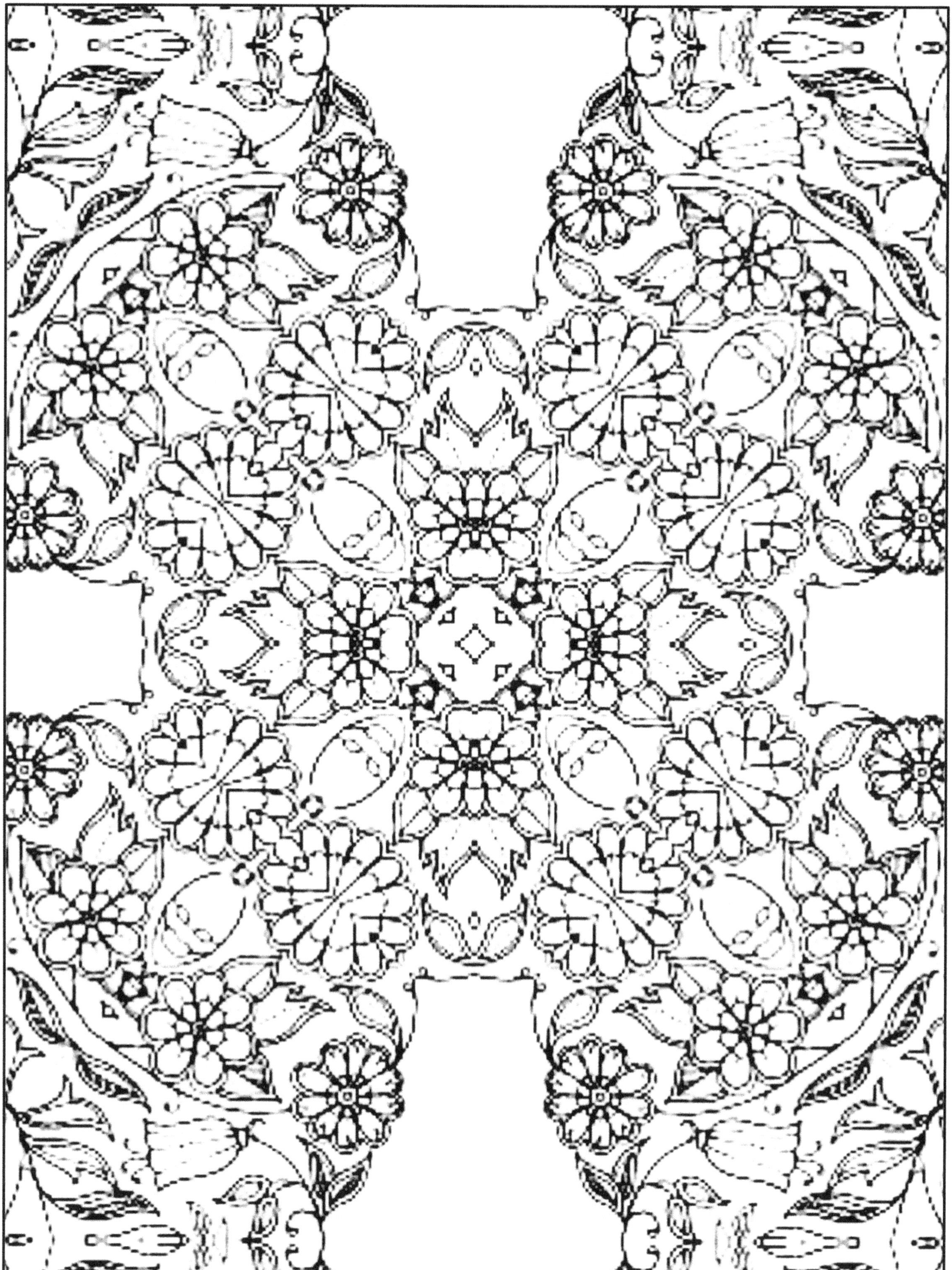

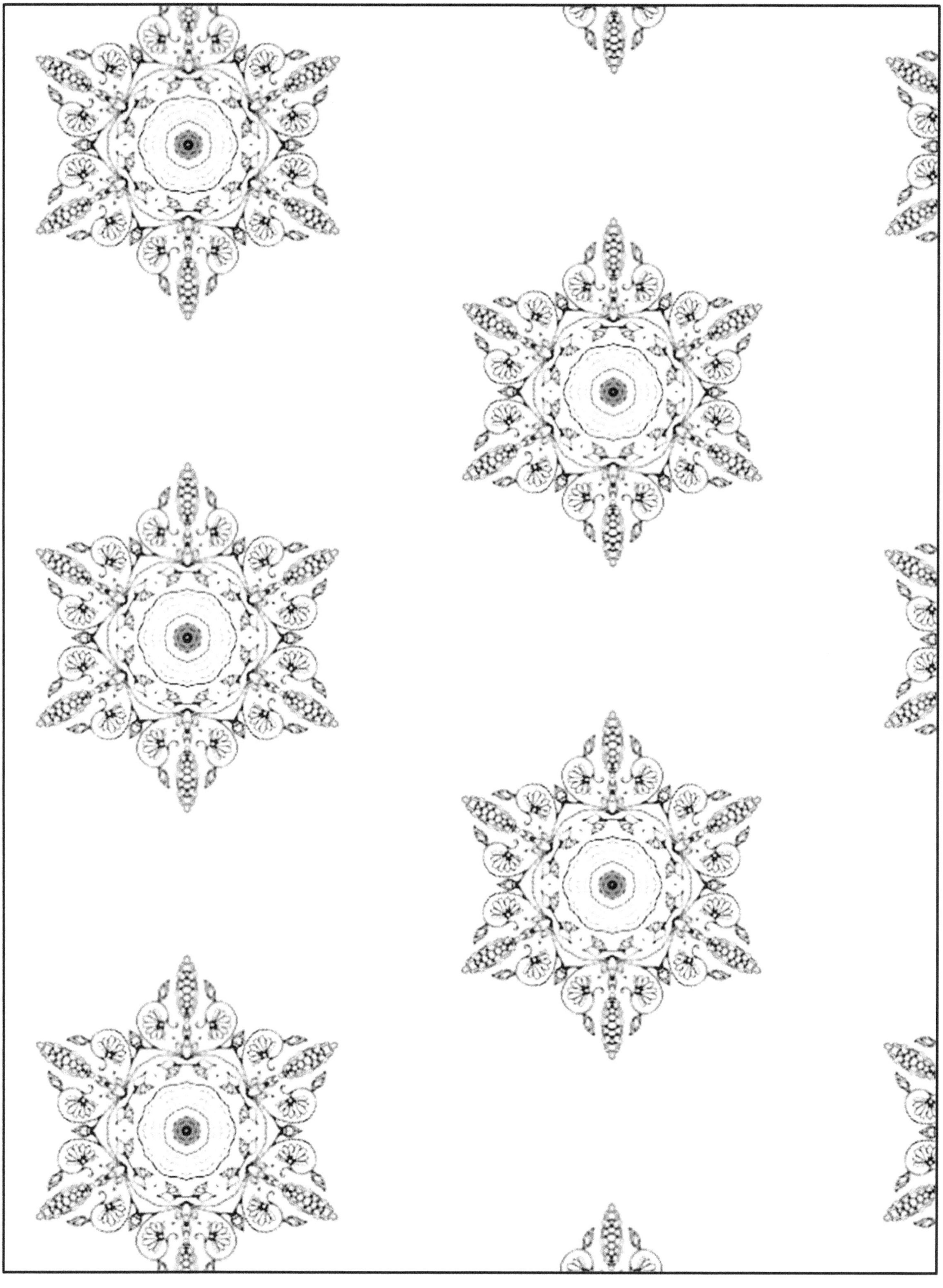

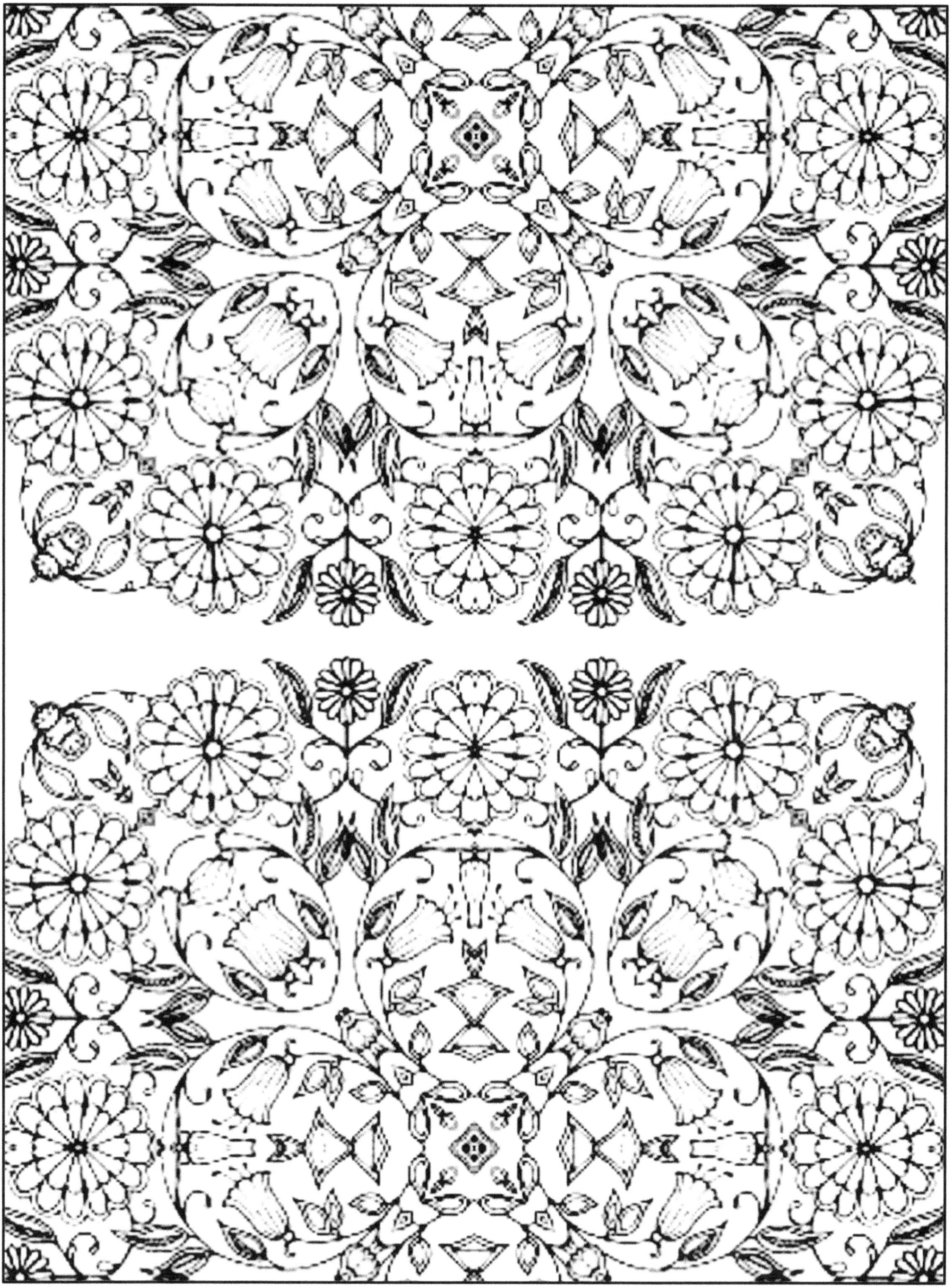

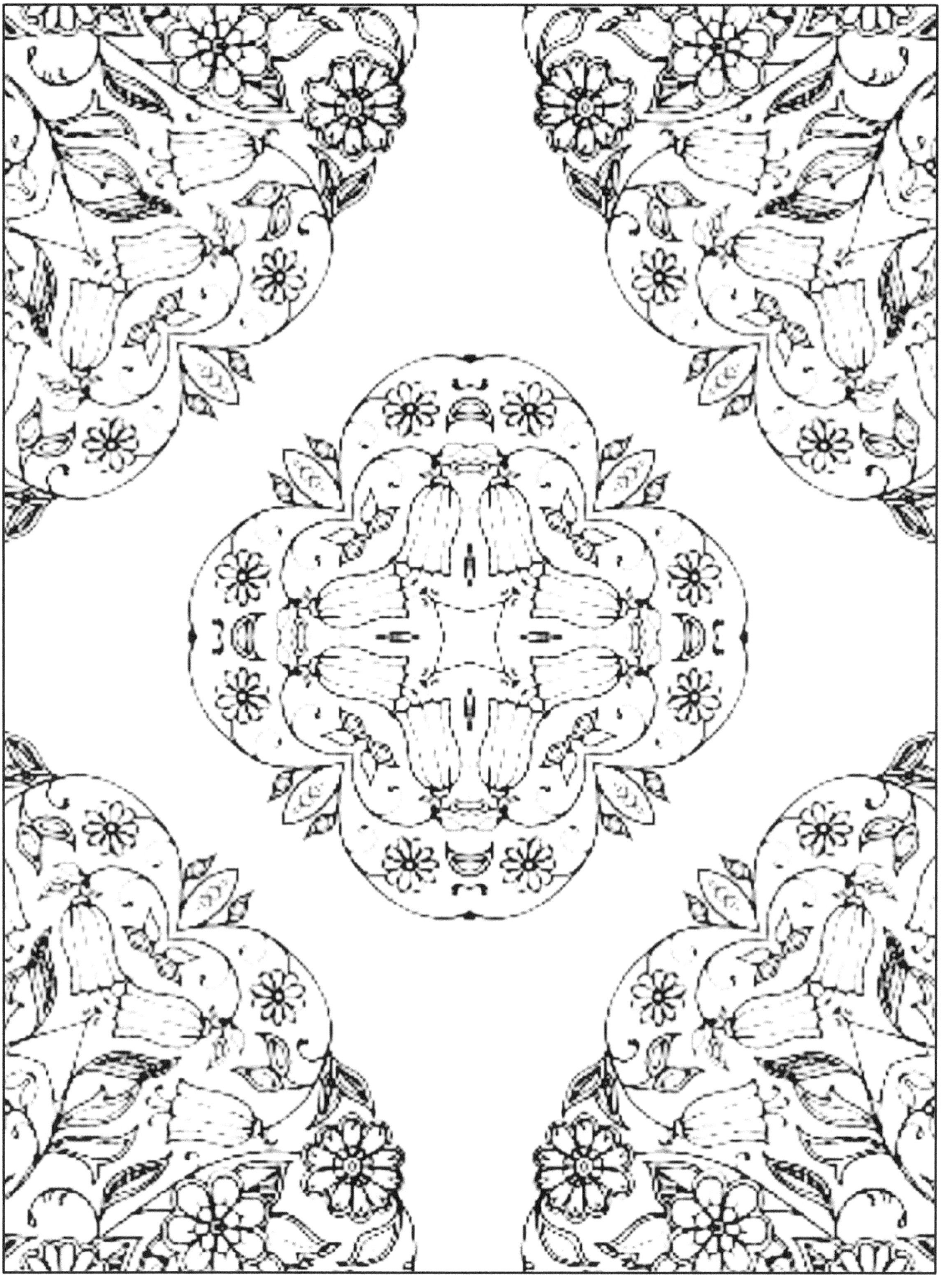

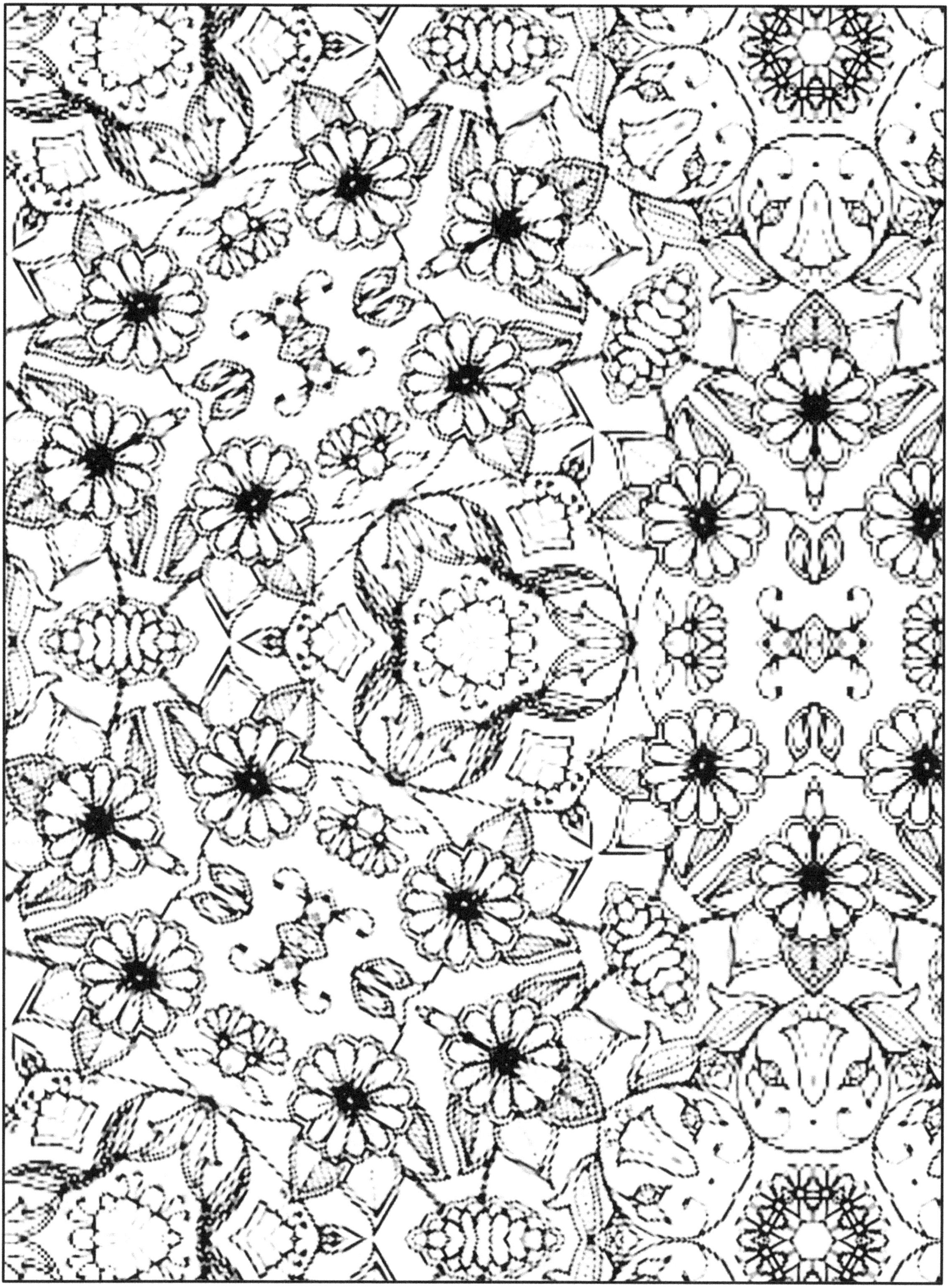

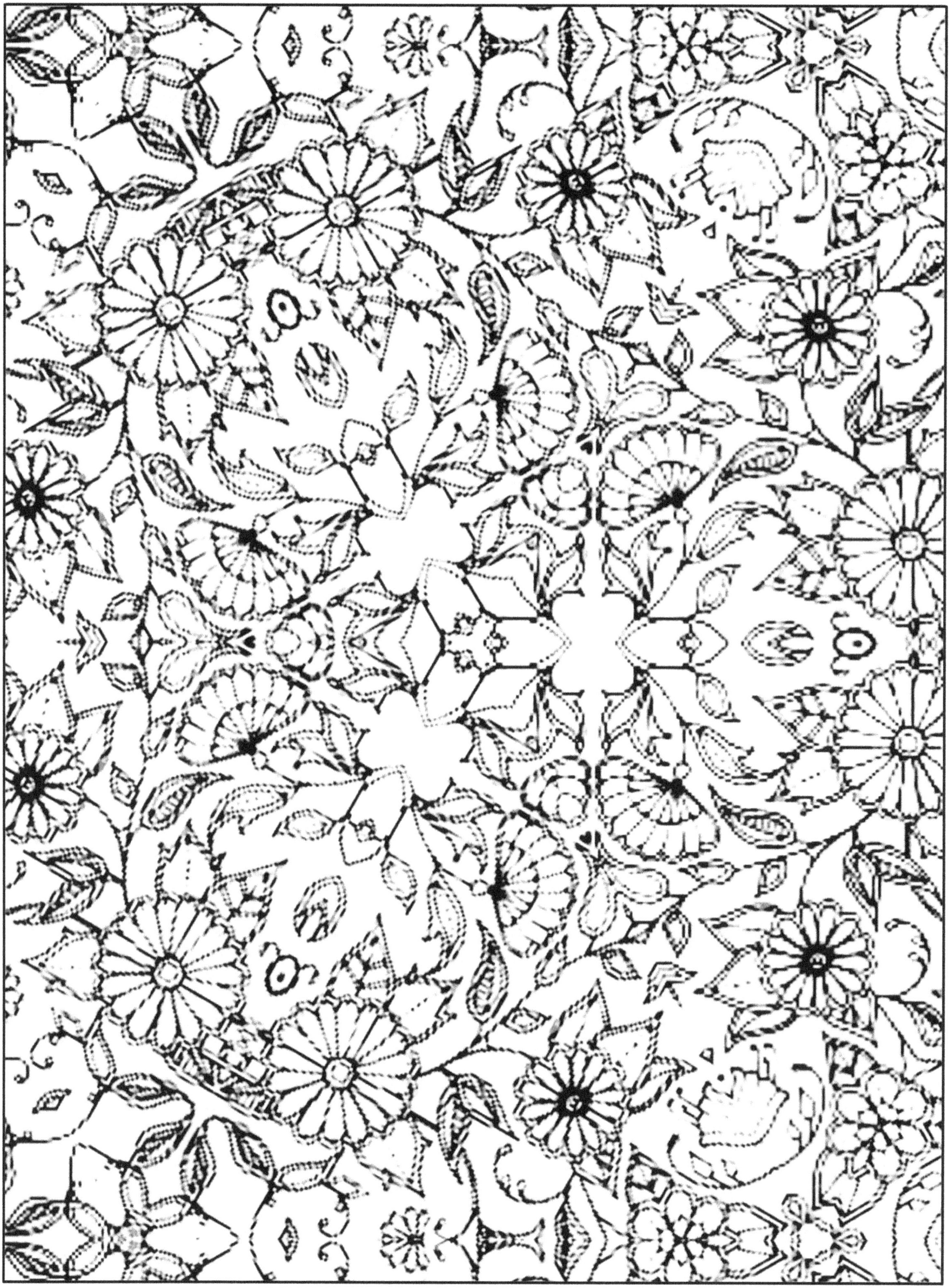

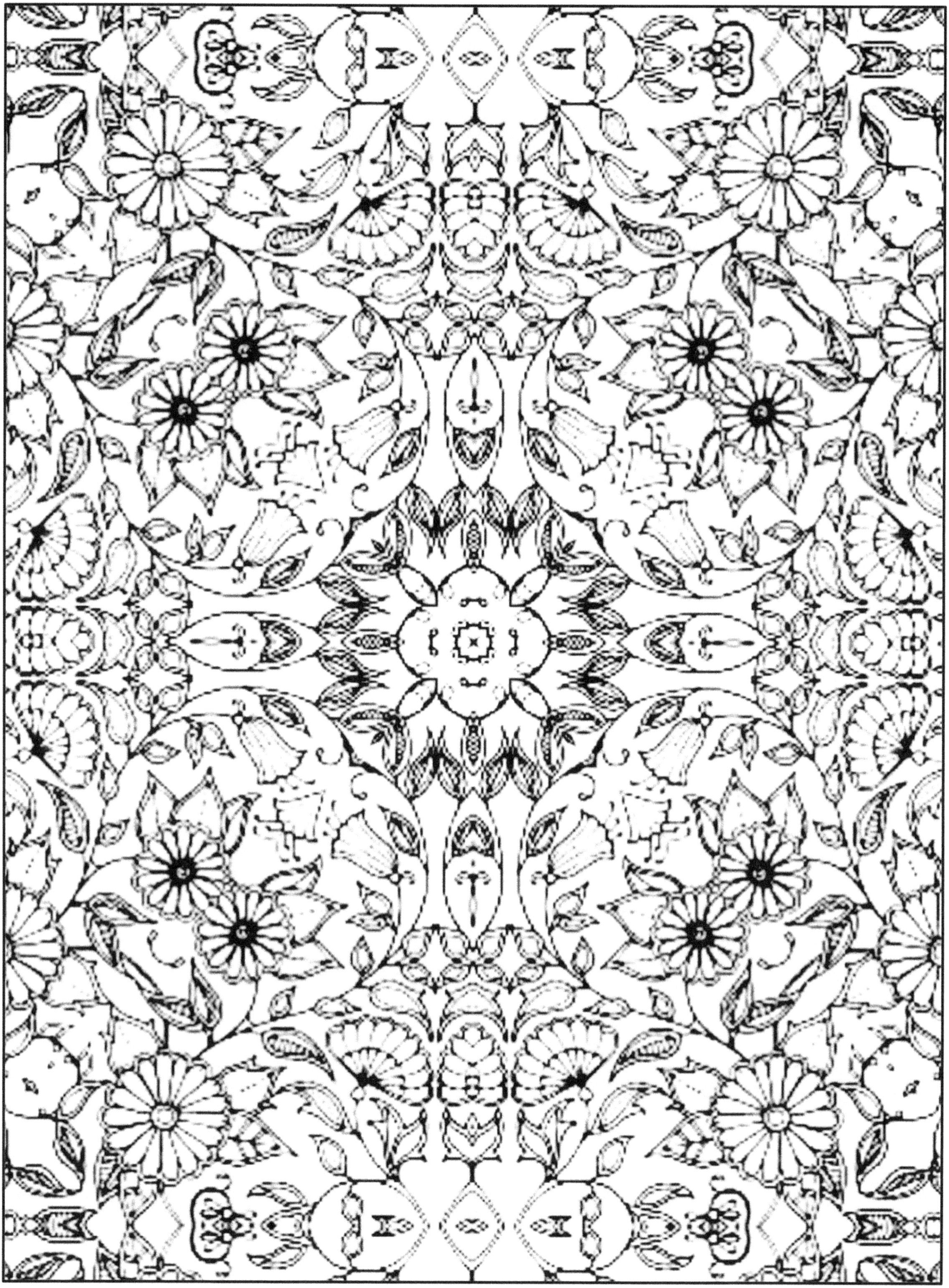

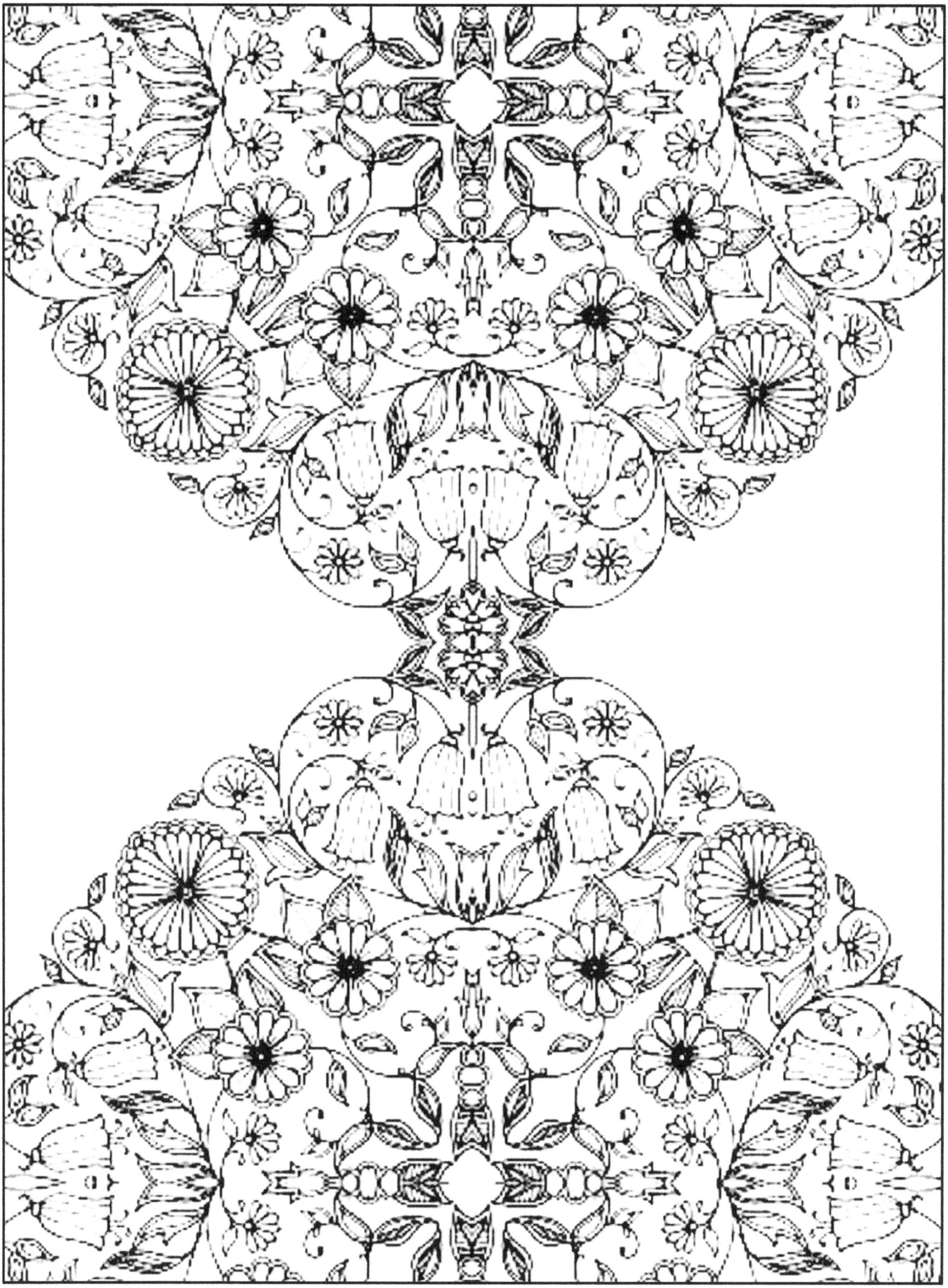

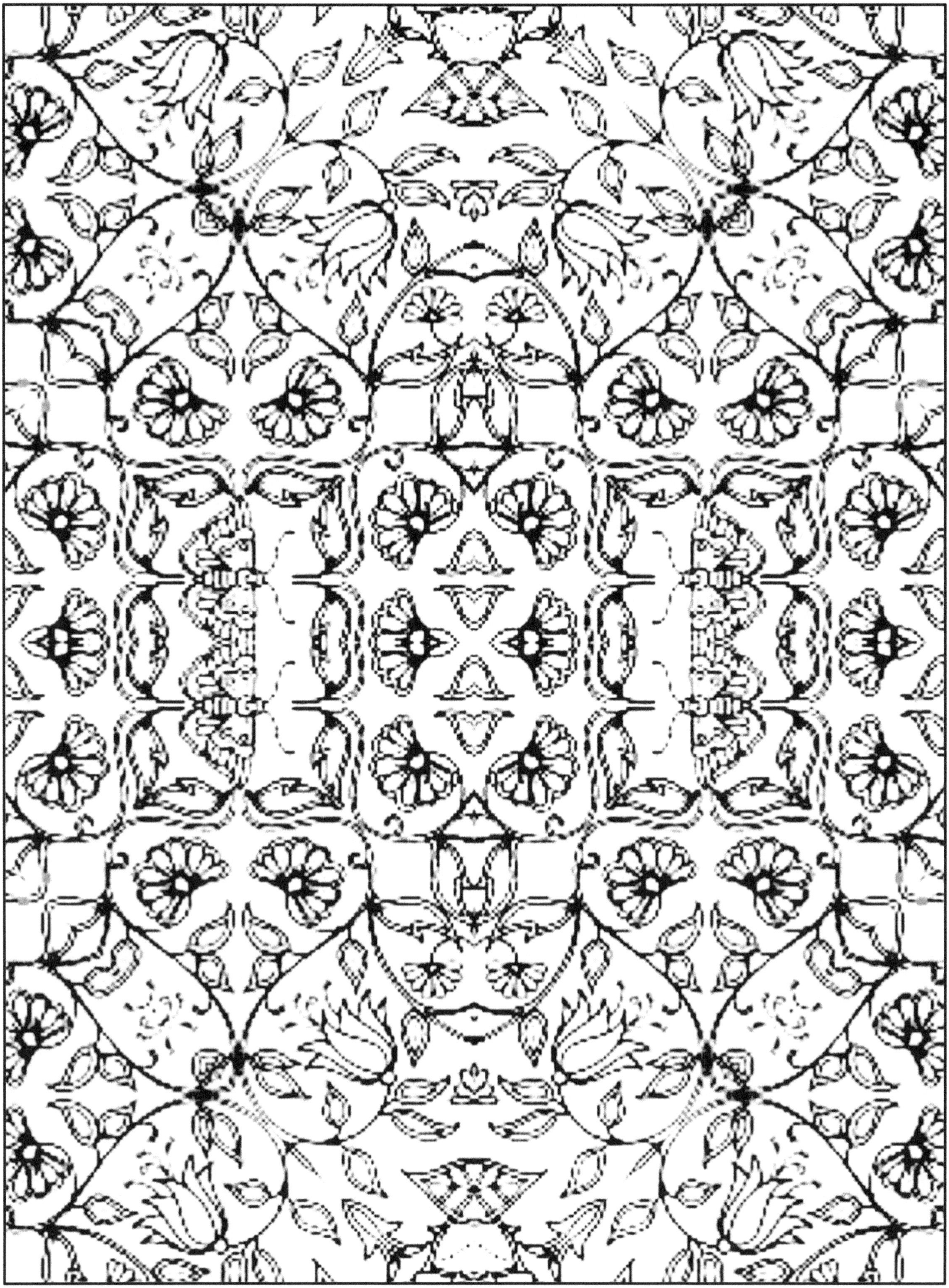

www.ingramcontent.com/pod-product-compliance
Lightning Source LLC
Chambersburg PA
CBHW080522190526
45169CB00008B/3023